I0797662

MANNERS ONLINE

by Emma Bassier

Cody Koala

An Imprint of Pop!
popbooksonline.com

abdobooks.com
Published by Pop!, a division of ABDO, PO Box 398166, Minneapolis, Minnesota 55439.

Printed in the United States of America, North Mankato, Minnesota

102019
012020

THIS BOOK CONTAINS RECYCLED MATERIALS

Cover Photo: iStockphoto
Interior Photos: iStockphoto, 1, 9, 11 (bottom right), 15, 16, 19 (top), 19 (bottom right), 21 (top right), 21 (bottom); Shutterstock Images, 5, 6, 7, 11 (top), 11 (bottom left), 12, 19 (bottom left), 21 (top left)

Editor: Brienna Rossiter
Series Designer: Jake Slavik

Library of Congress Control Number: 2019942781

Publisher's Cataloging-in-Publication Data
Names: Bassier, Emma, author.
Title: Manners online / by Emma Bassier
Description: Minneapolis, Minnesota : Pop!, 2020 | Series: Manners matter | Includes online resources and index.
Identifiers: ISBN 9781532165658 (lib. bdg.) | ISBN 9781644942987 (pbk.) | ISBN 9781532166976 (ebook)
Subjects: LCSH: Manners--Juvenile literature. | Polite behavior--Juvenile literature. | Internet and children--Juvenile literature. | Social customs--Juvenile literature. | Netiquette--Juvenile literature.
Classification: DDC 395.12--dc23

Hello! My name is

Cody Koala

Pop open this book and you'll find QR codes like this one, loaded with information, so you can learn even more!

Scan this code* and others like it while you read, or visit the website below to make this book pop.

popbooksonline.com/manners-online

*Scanning QR codes requires a web-enabled smart device with a QR code reader app and a camera.

Table of Contents

Chapter 1

Thinking of Others

A girl messages her friend online. She thinks about teasing him with a friendly joke. But that might hurt his feelings. So, she sends a smiley face instead.

Watch a video here!

People use the internet to **interact** in many ways. They can send messages. They can also see and like posts.

A post is words or images that someone puts online. Sometimes people comment on posts. They share their thoughts.

Often, people can't see the people they interact with online. As a result, **manners** can seem less important. People may be tempted to post things they would never say in person. But good manners help people remember to think of how others might feel.

In 2018, eight out of ten people in the United States went online every day.

Chapter 2

Use Kind Words

Polite people are careful about what they say online. They don't **gossip**. And they avoid putting other people down, even as a joke.

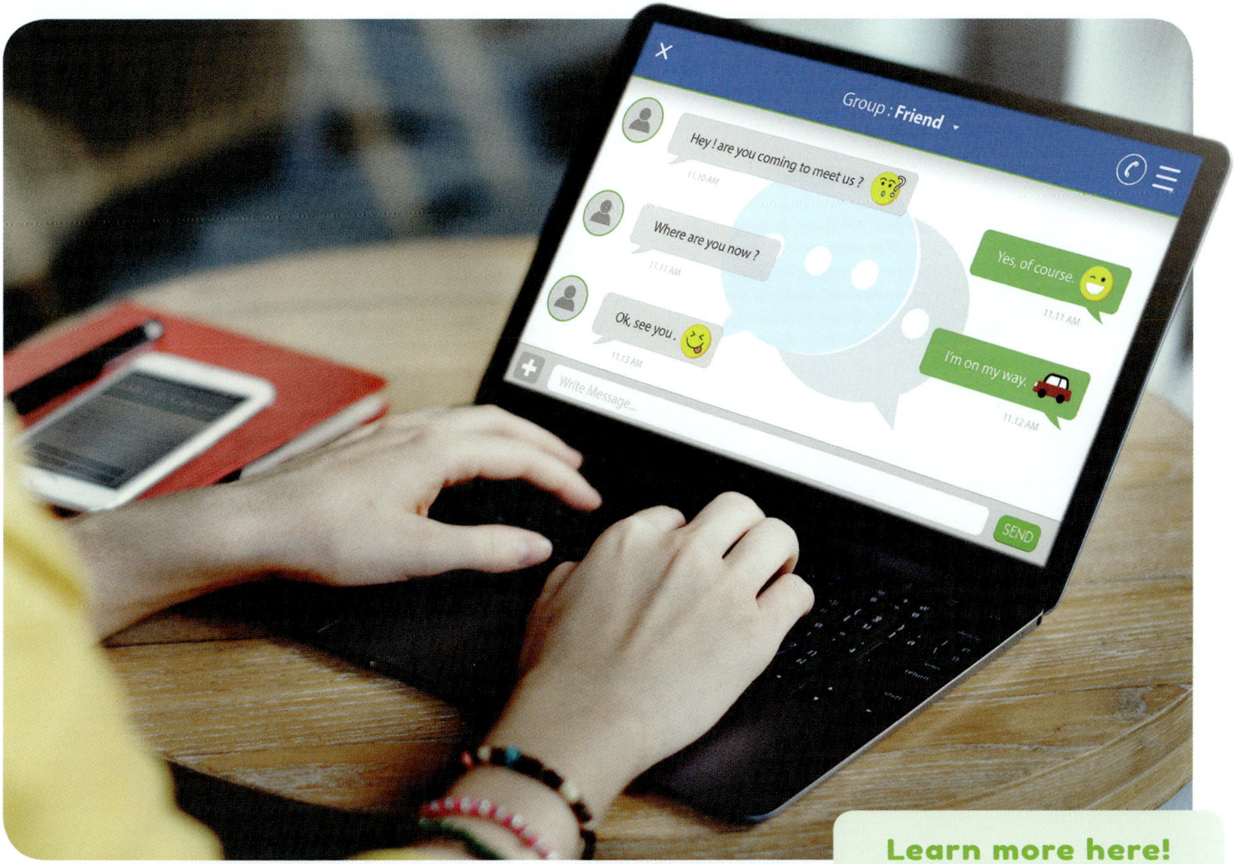

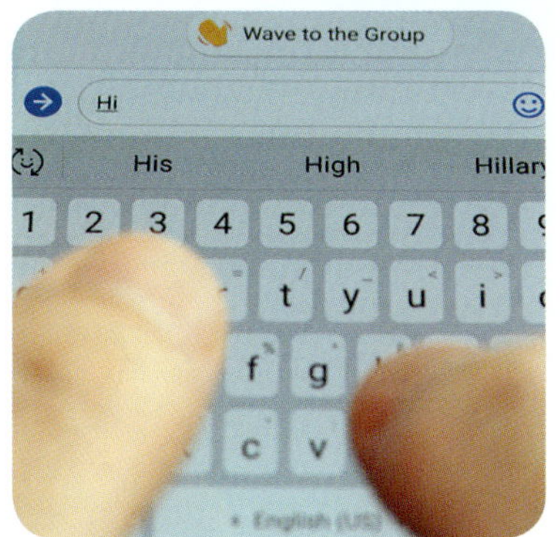

Learn more here!

It is important to show **respect**. Always use kind words, even if someone doesn’t agree with you. When writing a message, think about how you would feel if someone said it to you.

Using all capital letters can show excitement. But many people think it is the same as shouting.

Chapter 3

Stop and Think

When information is online, many people can see it. It can spread quickly. Often, it can't be taken back. For this reason, people must be careful about what they post.

Complete an
activity here!

People should stop and think before posting. A pause gives time for strong emotions to calm down. That way, people are less likely to post something they will **regret**.

Chapter 4

When to Go Online

People show good **manners** by thinking about when to go online. In quiet places, people should use headphones or put devices away.

Learn more here!

Using a device when you're with others can make them feel unimportant. Instead, give people your full attention. Doing this helps show them **respect** and care.

Wait before posting.

Use kind words.

Think how others might feel.

Making Connections

Text-to-Self

Have you ever read a mean comment online? How did it make you feel?

Text-to-Text

Have you read other books about manners? What did you learn?

Text-to-World

People can show manners by putting devices away when spending time with others. How might this make others feel?

Glossary

gossip – to say unkind words about other people without them knowing.

interact – to share a conversation or experience.

manners – the correct words or actions for certain situations.

polite – showing good manners.

regret – to feel sadness or wish you had not done something.

respect – a way of treating others that shows you care about their thoughts and feelings.

Index

Online Resources

popbooksonline.com

Thanks for reading this Cody Koala book!

Scan this code* and others like it in this book, or visit the website below to make this book pop!

popbooksonline.com/manners-online

*Scanning QR codes requires a web-enabled smart device with a QR code reader app and a camera.